EASY MANDALA Coloring Book

For

Grandma

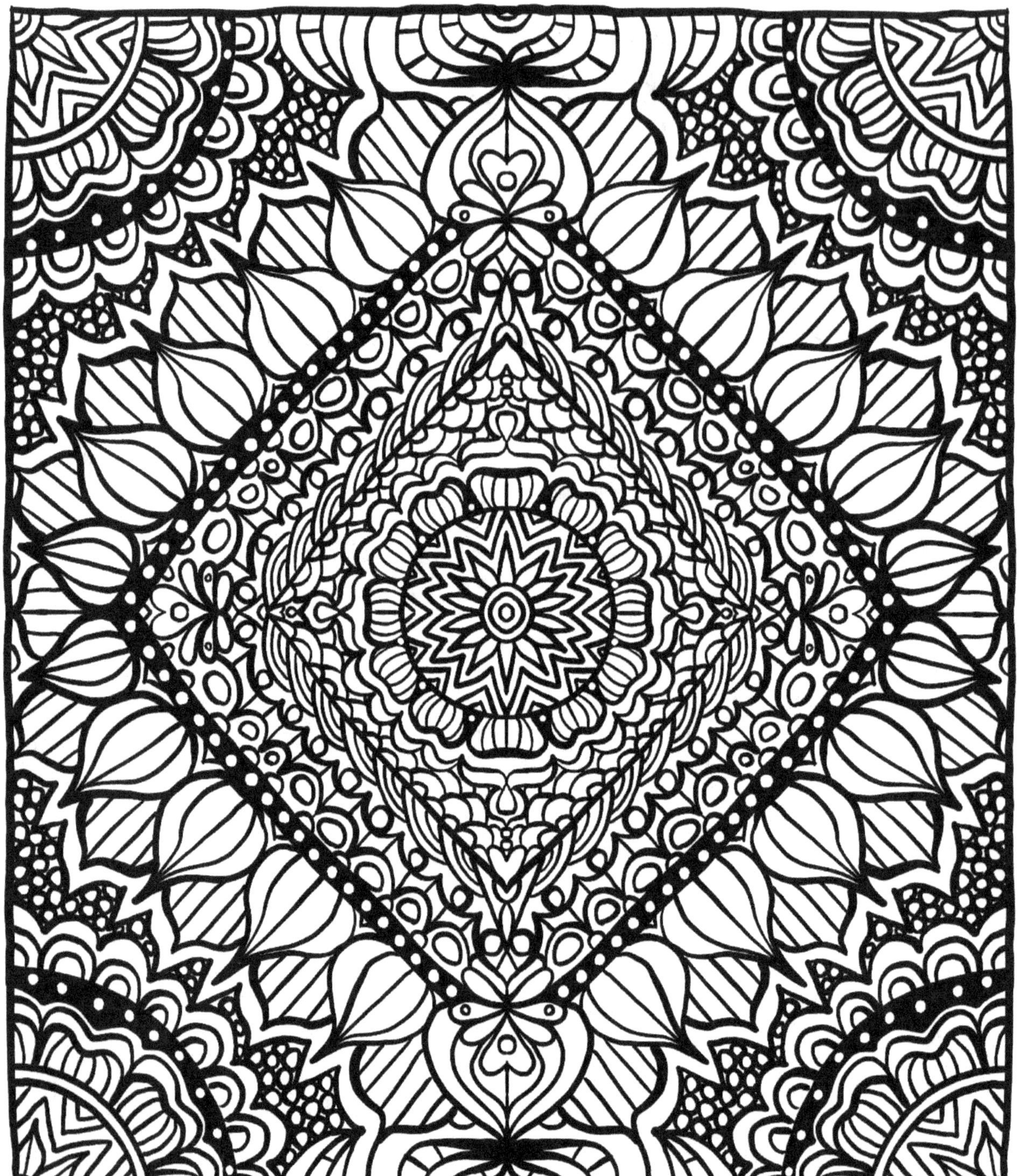

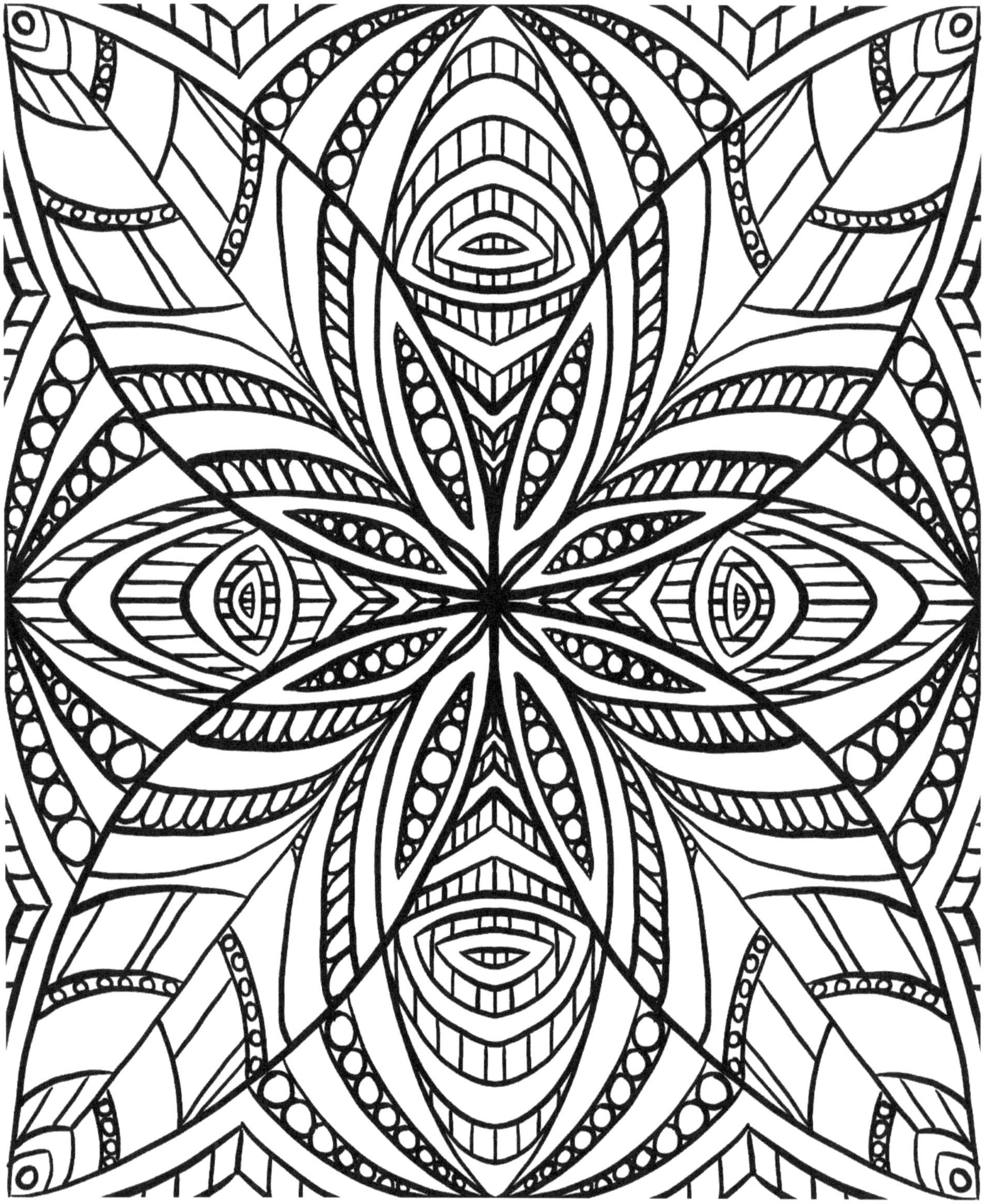

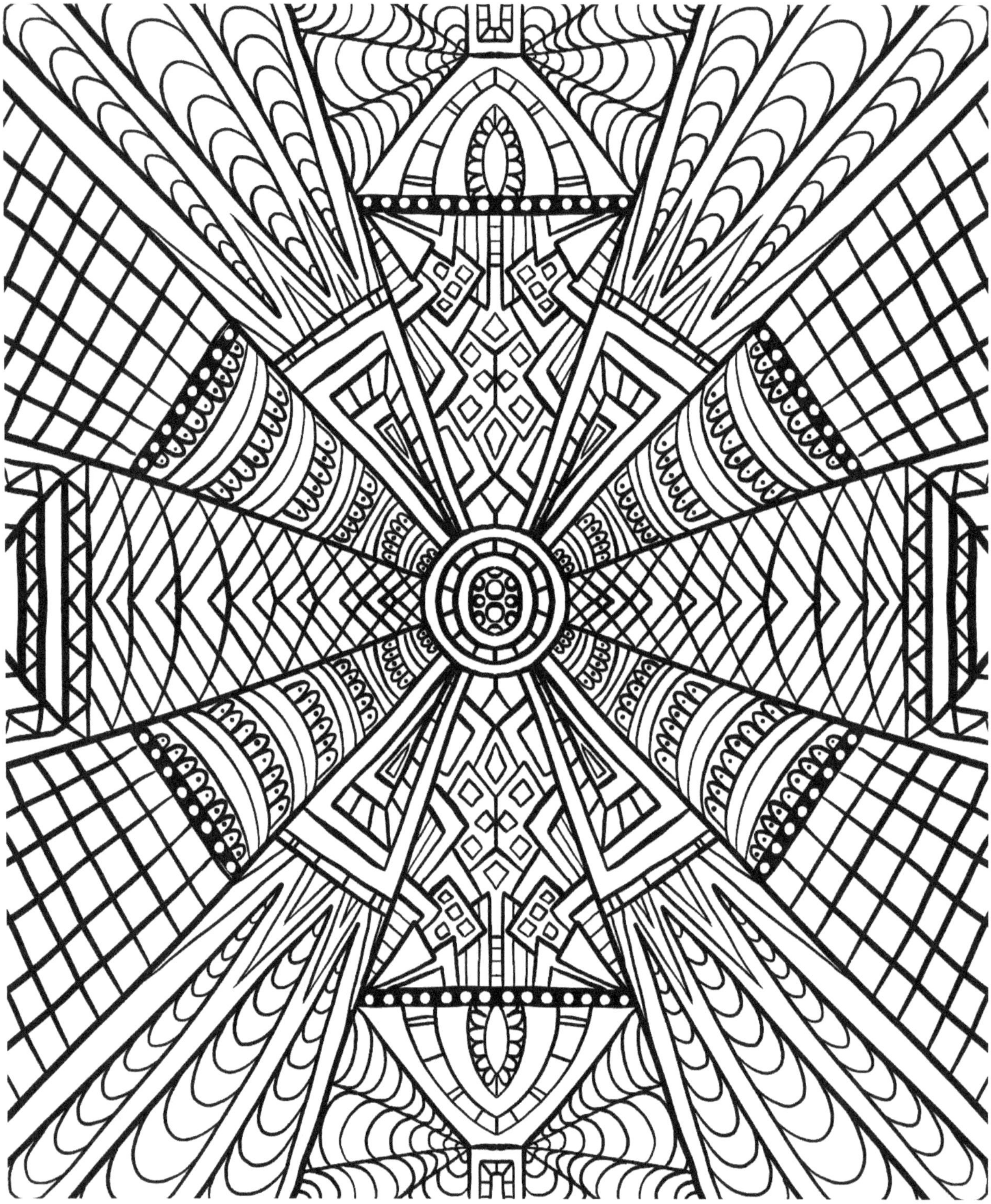

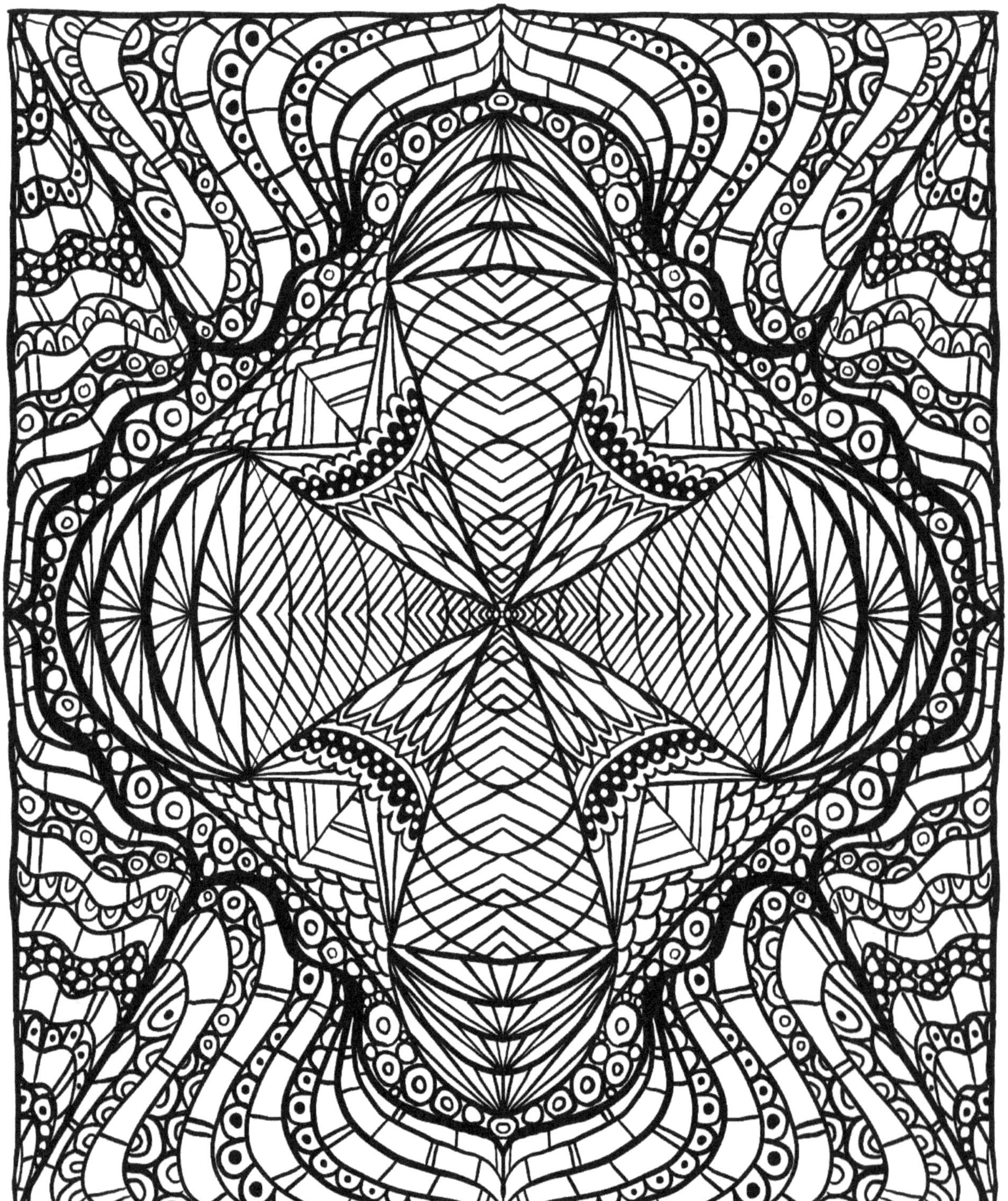

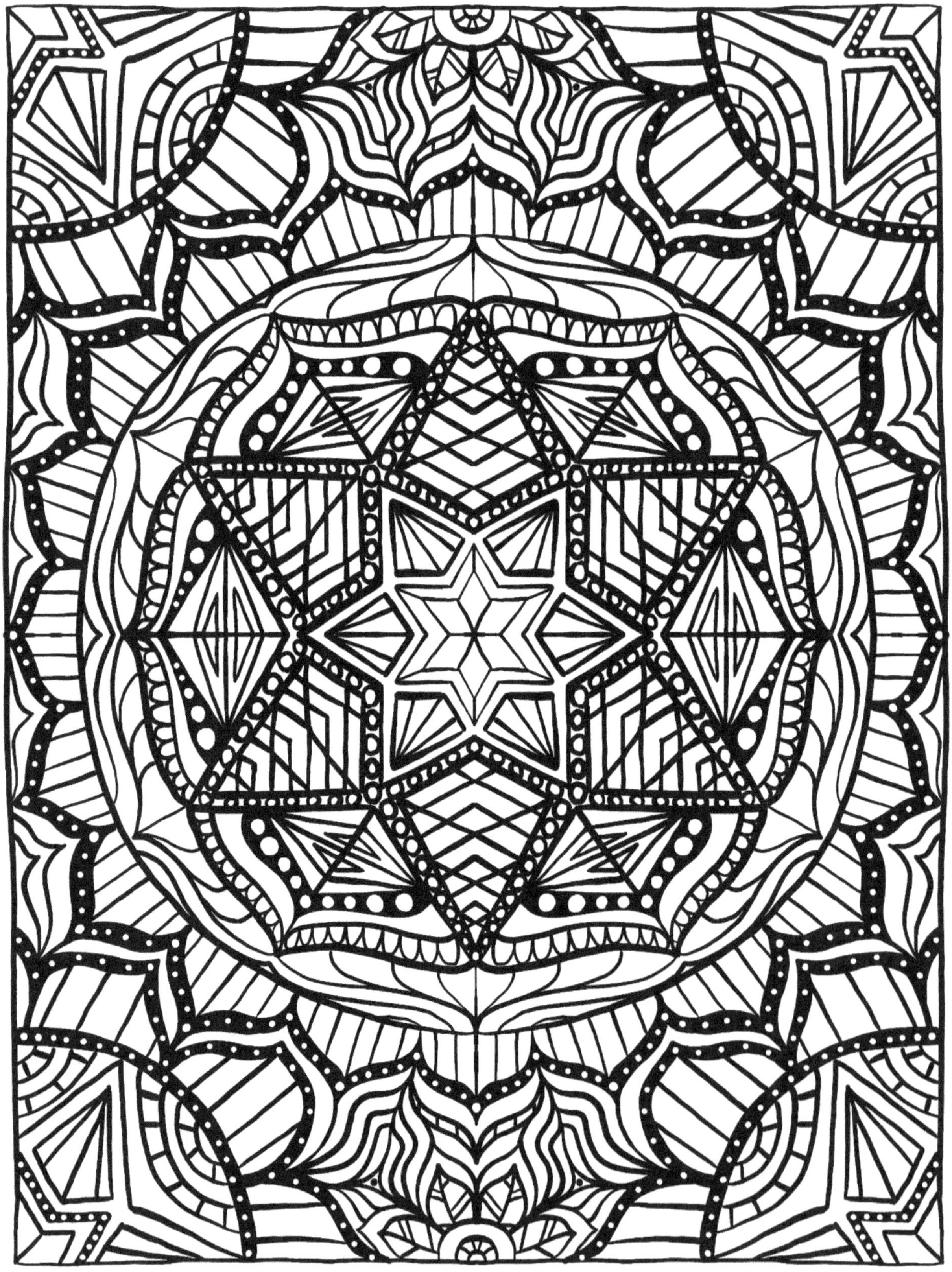

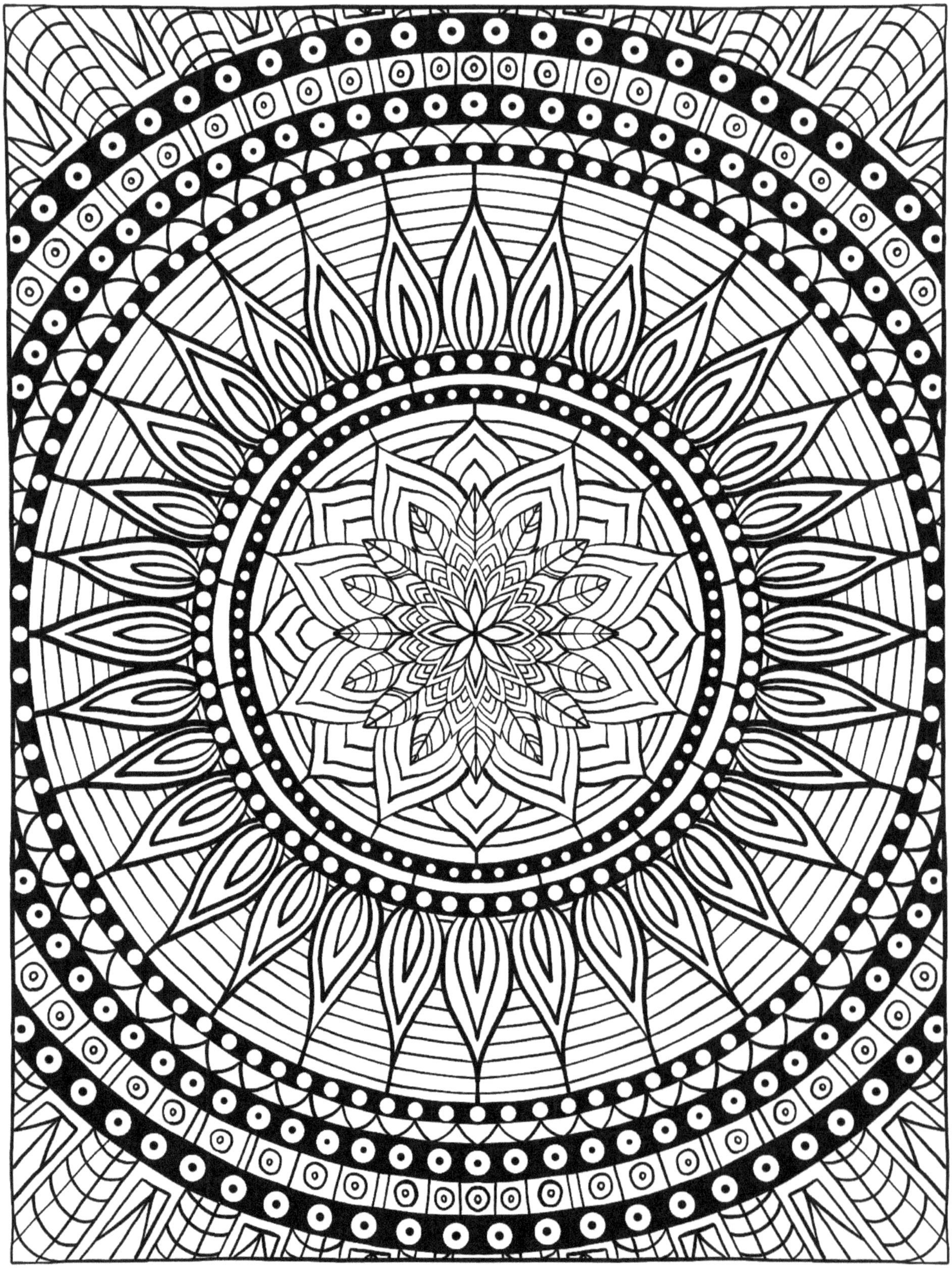

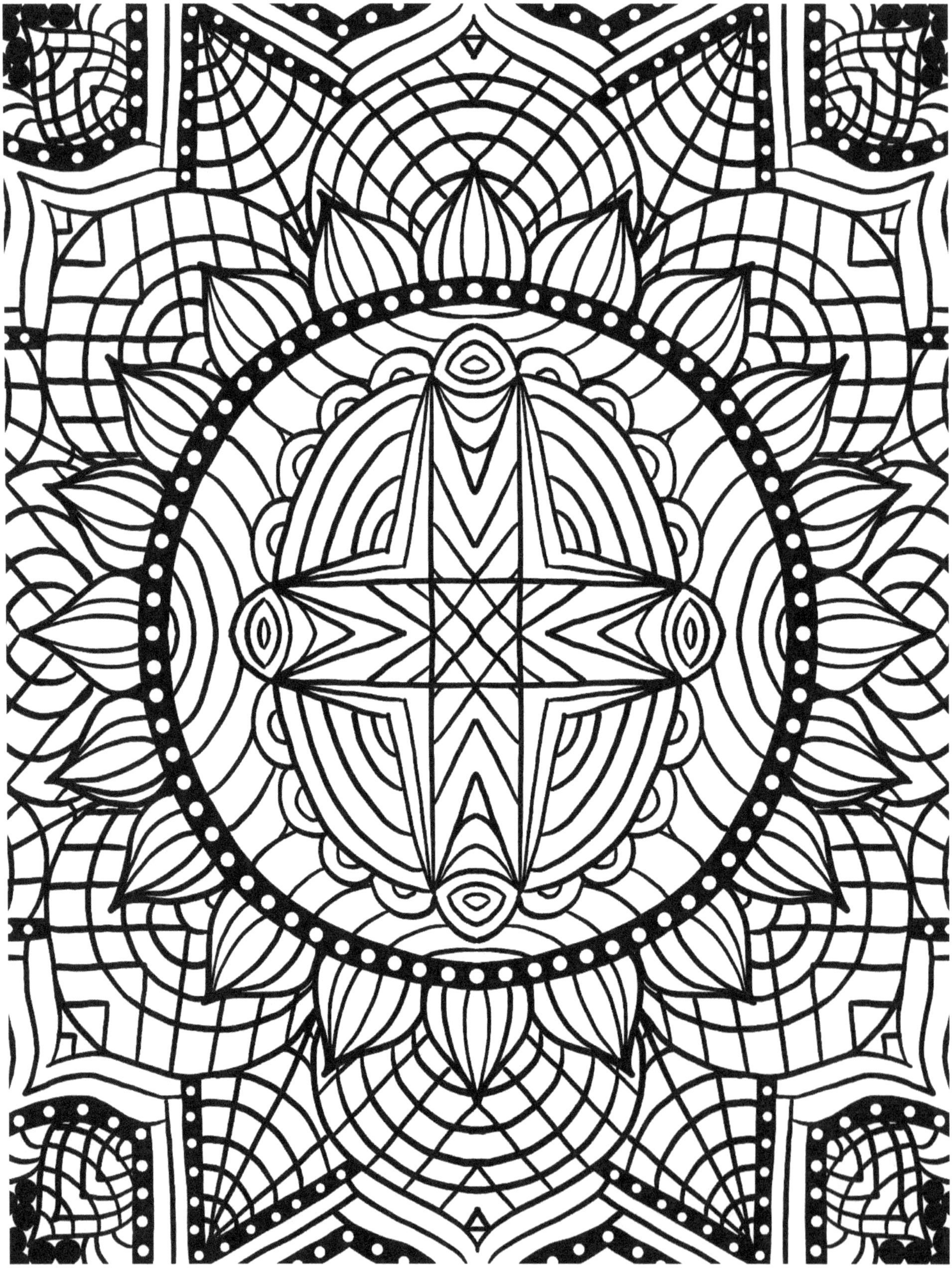

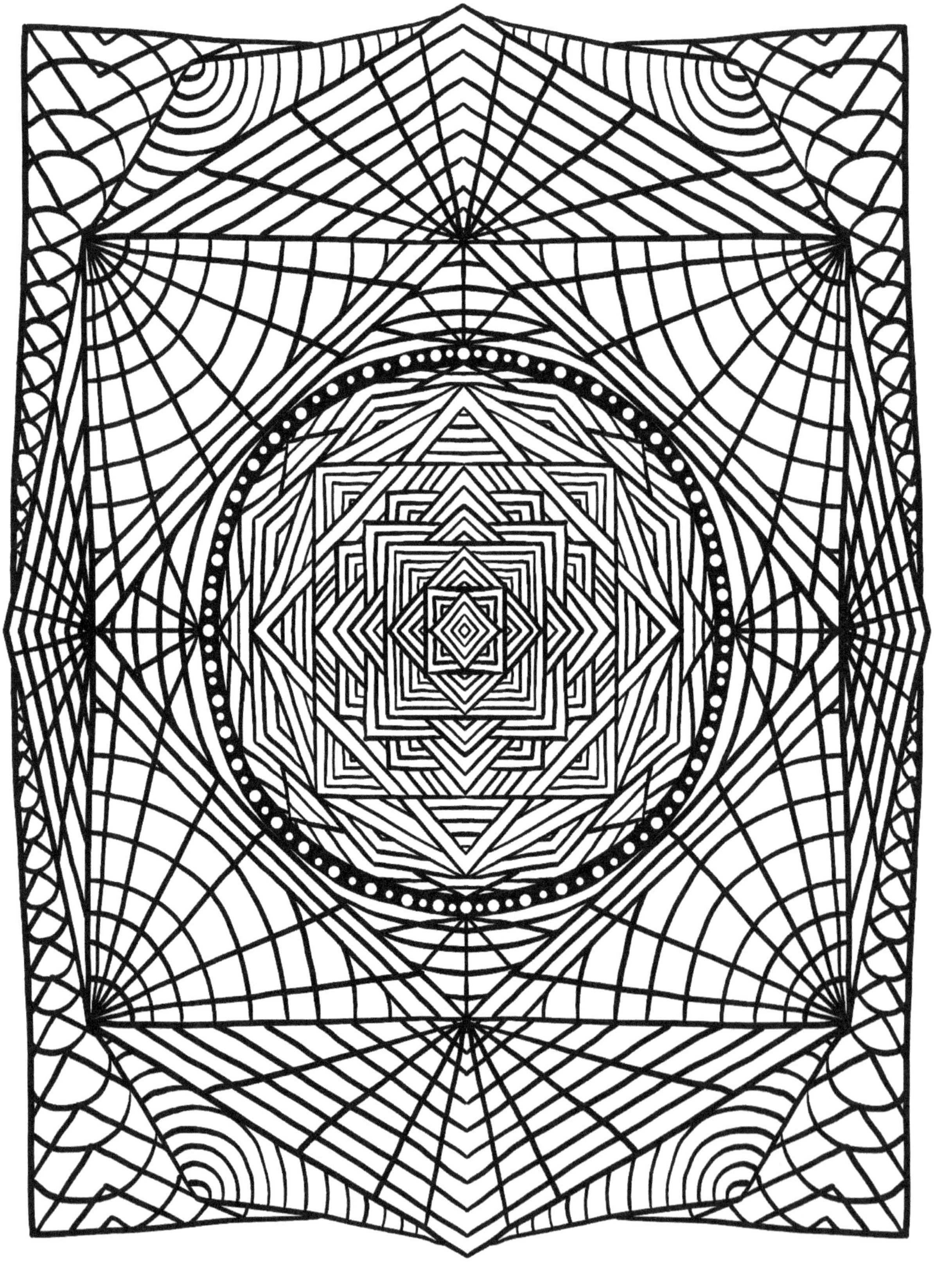

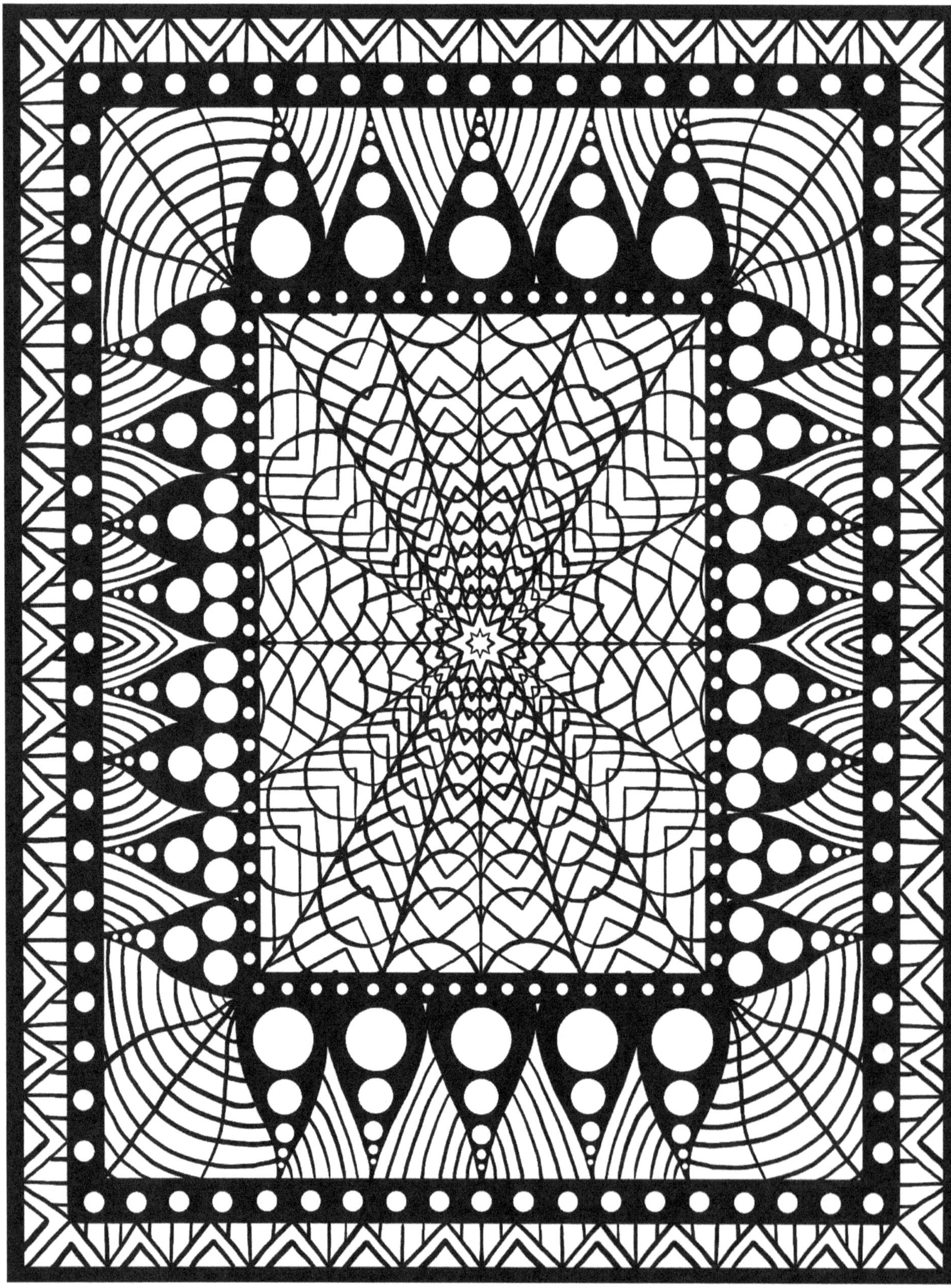

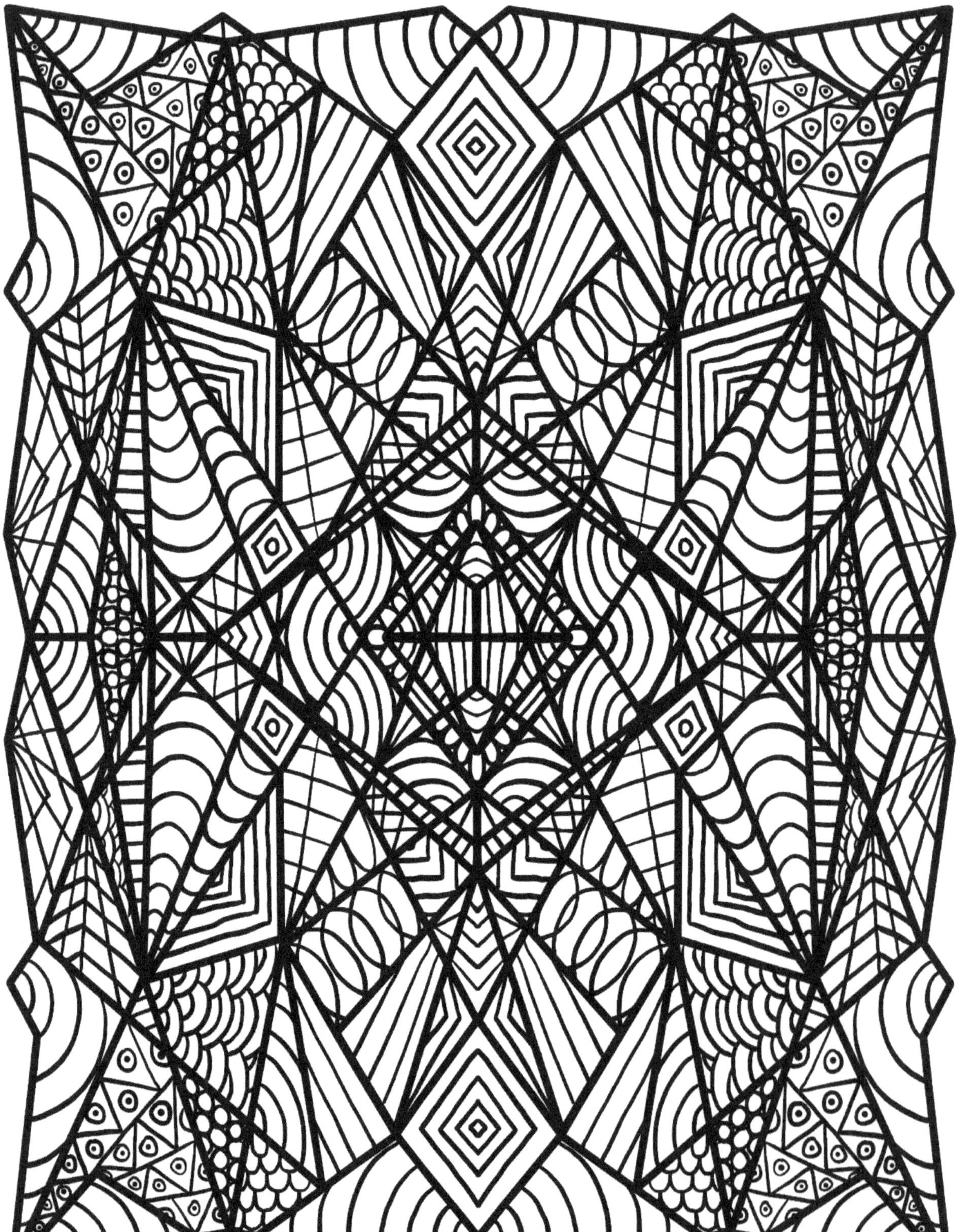

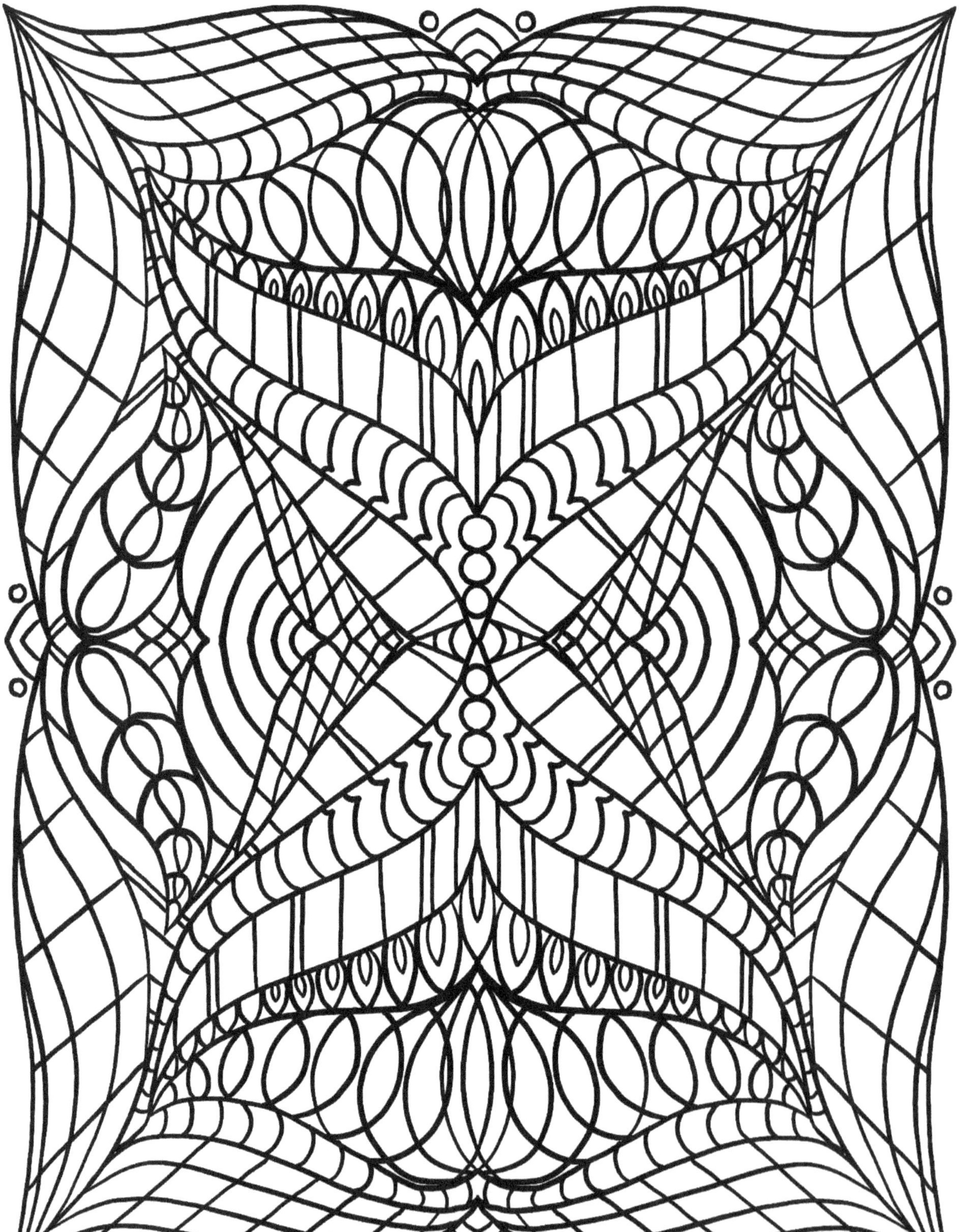

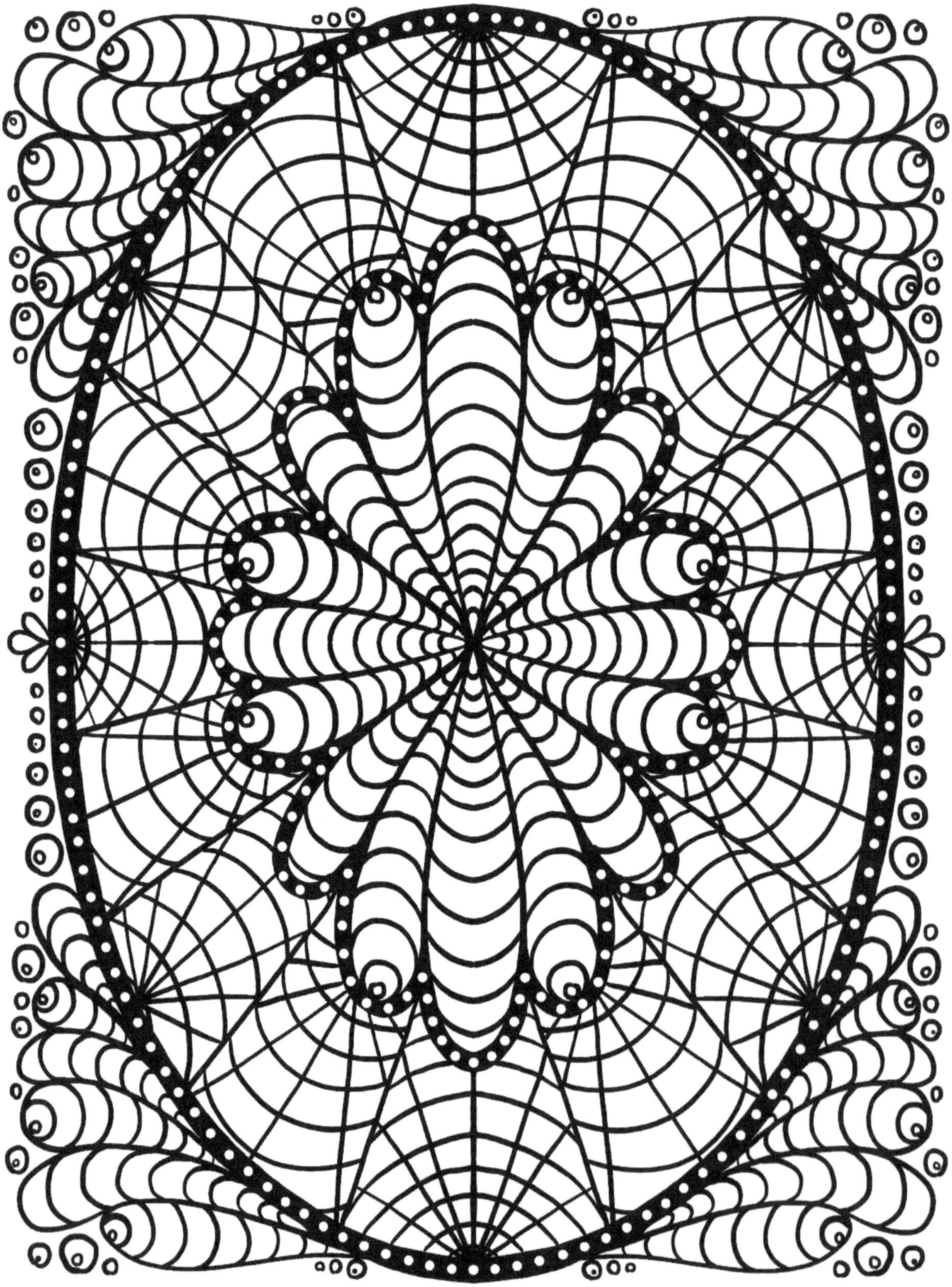

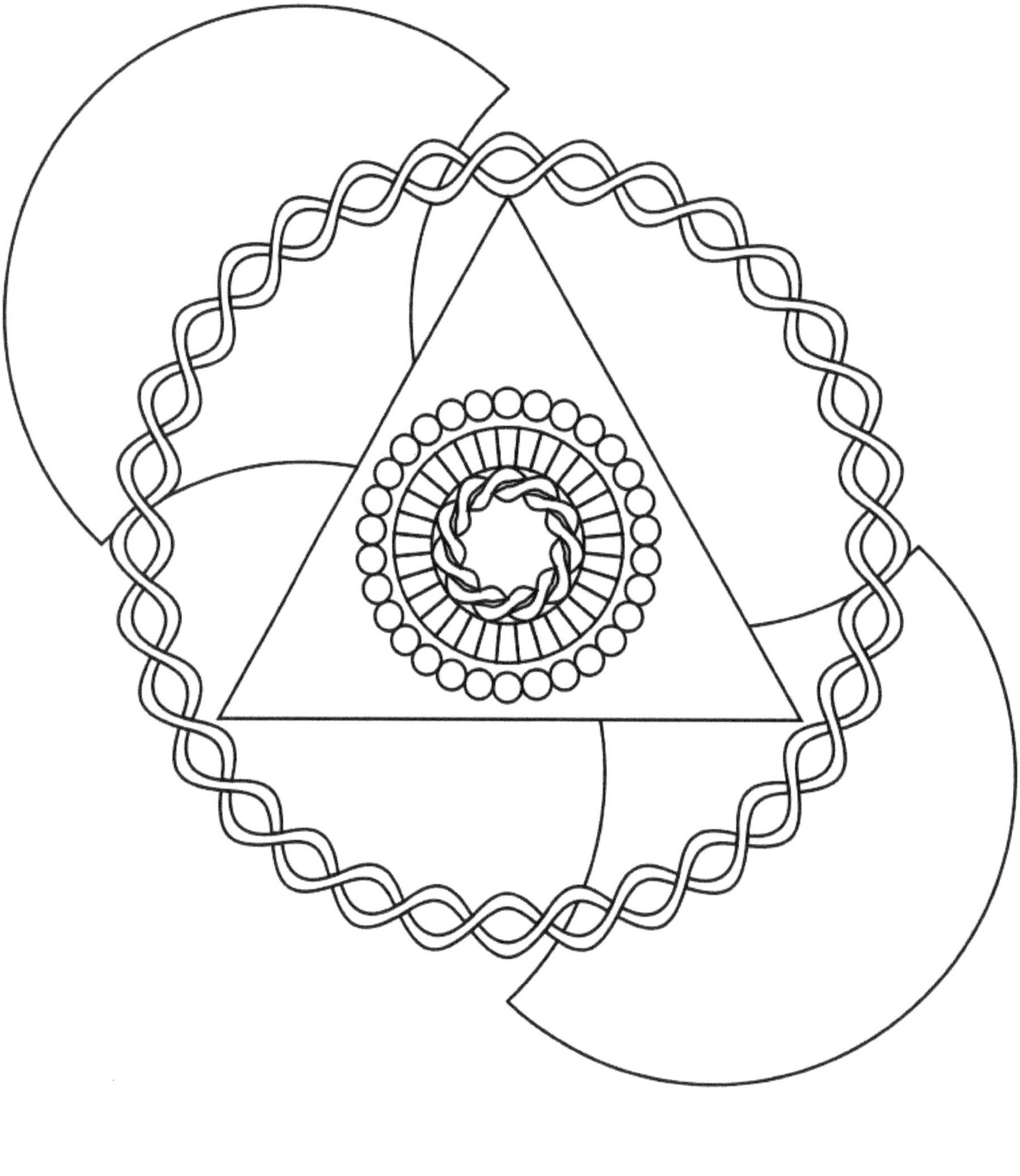

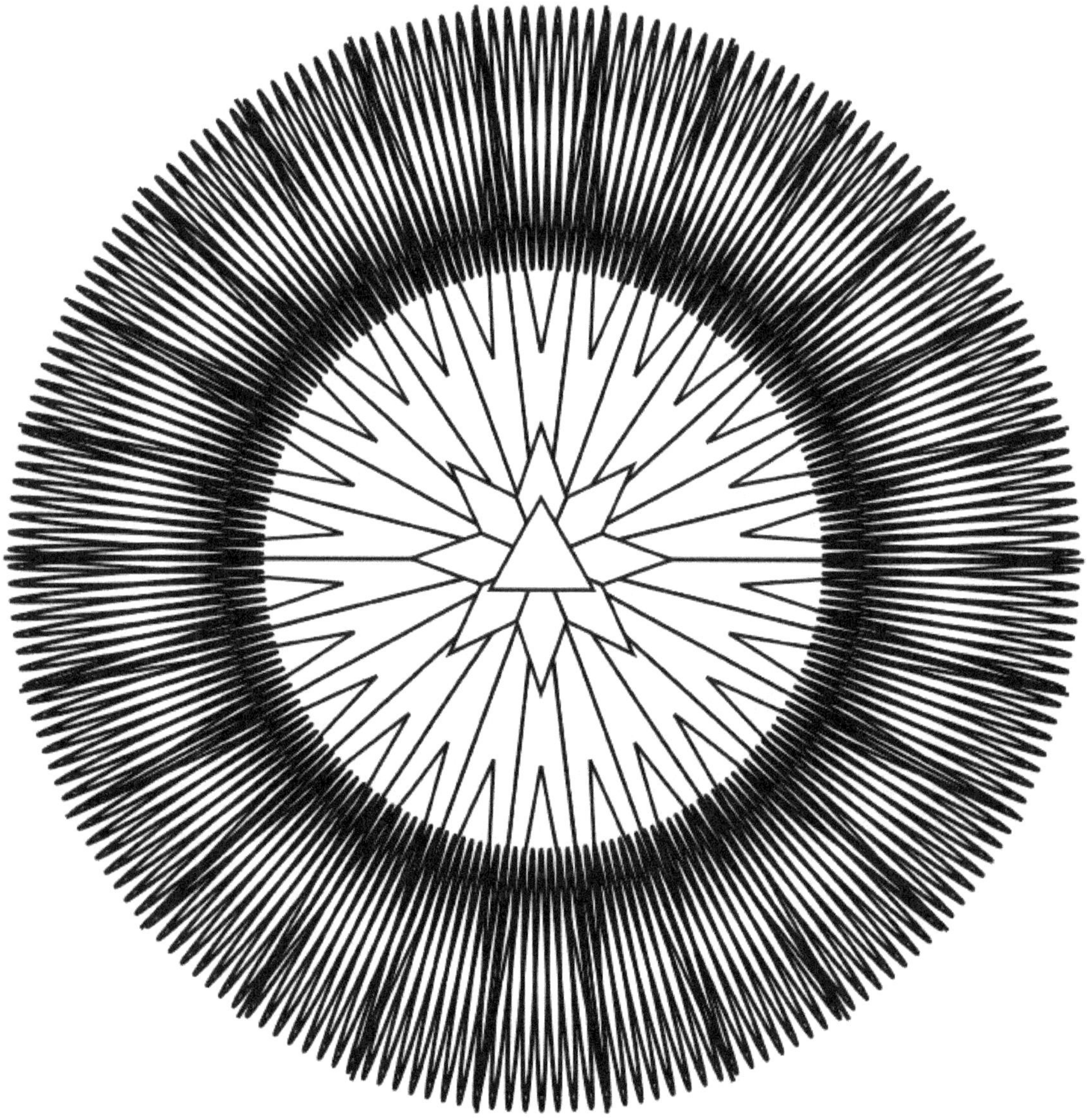

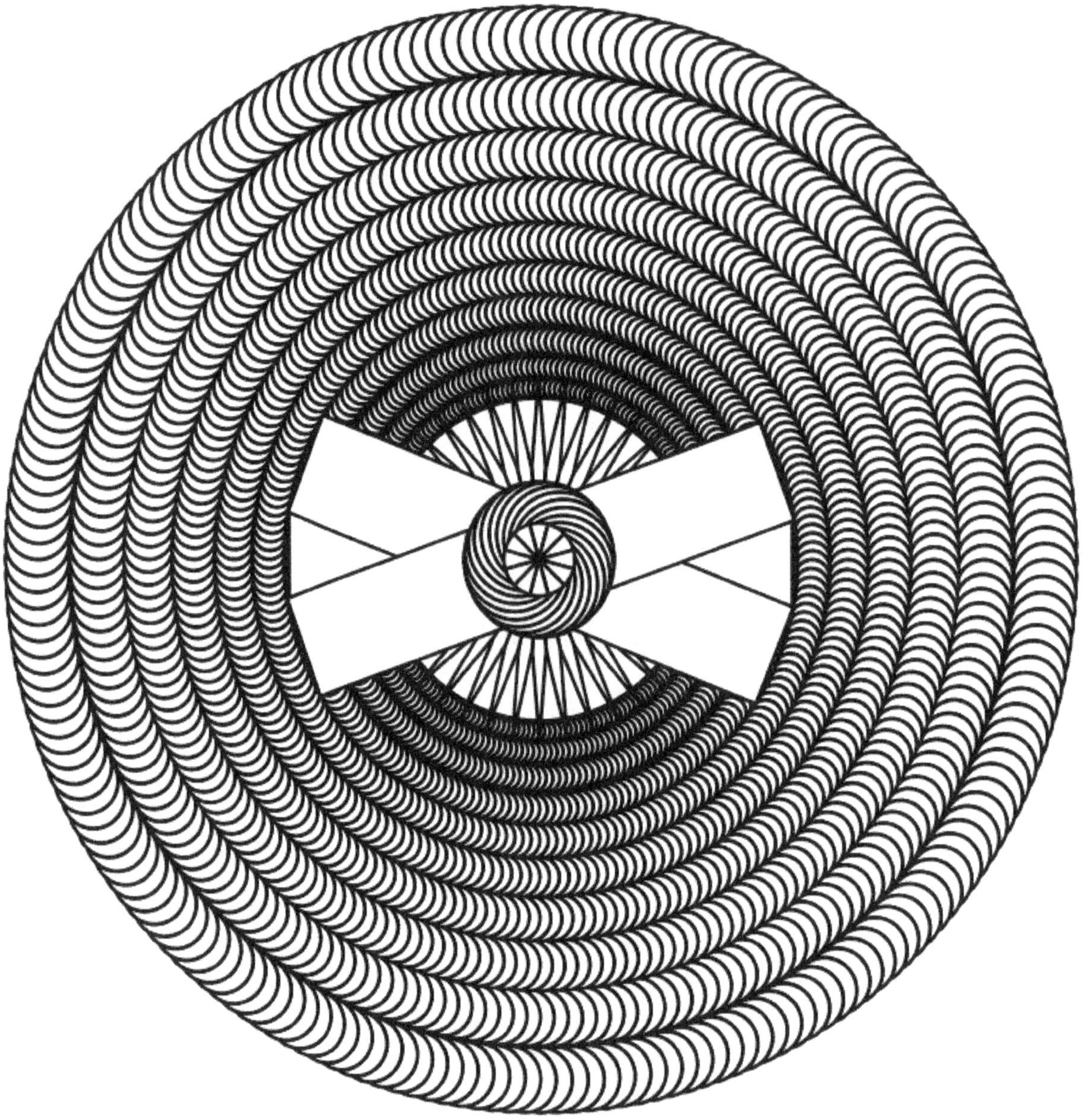

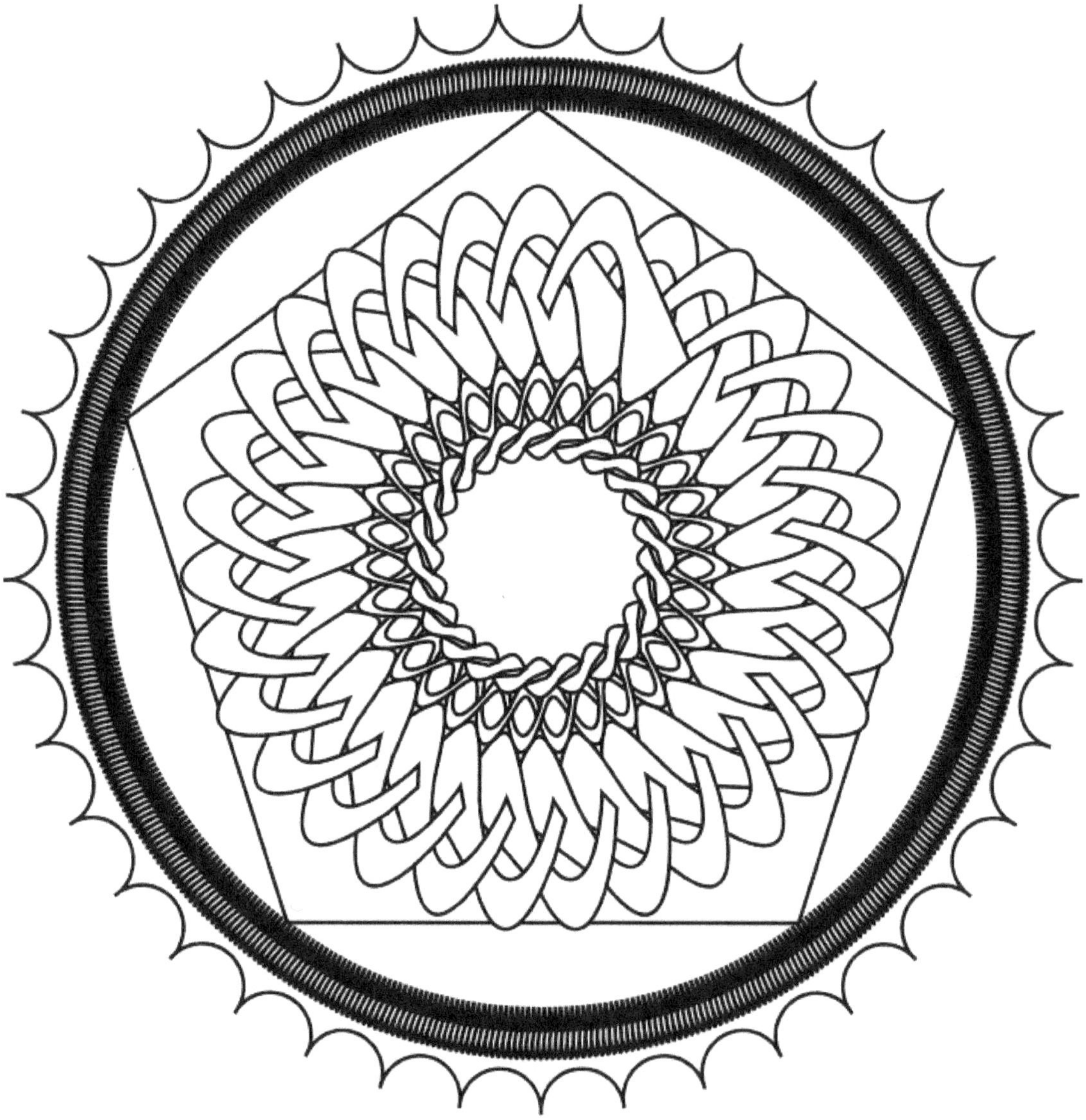

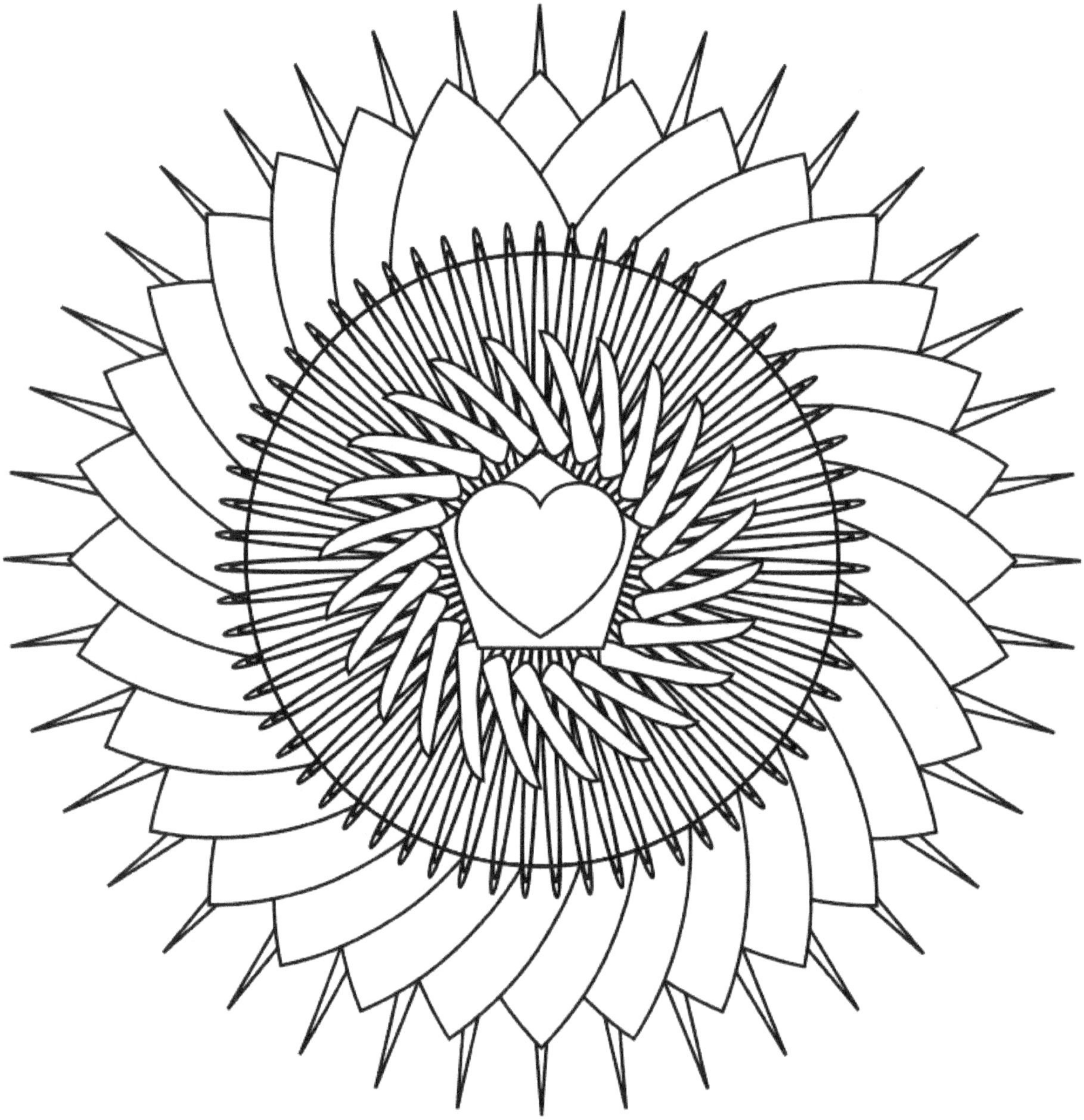

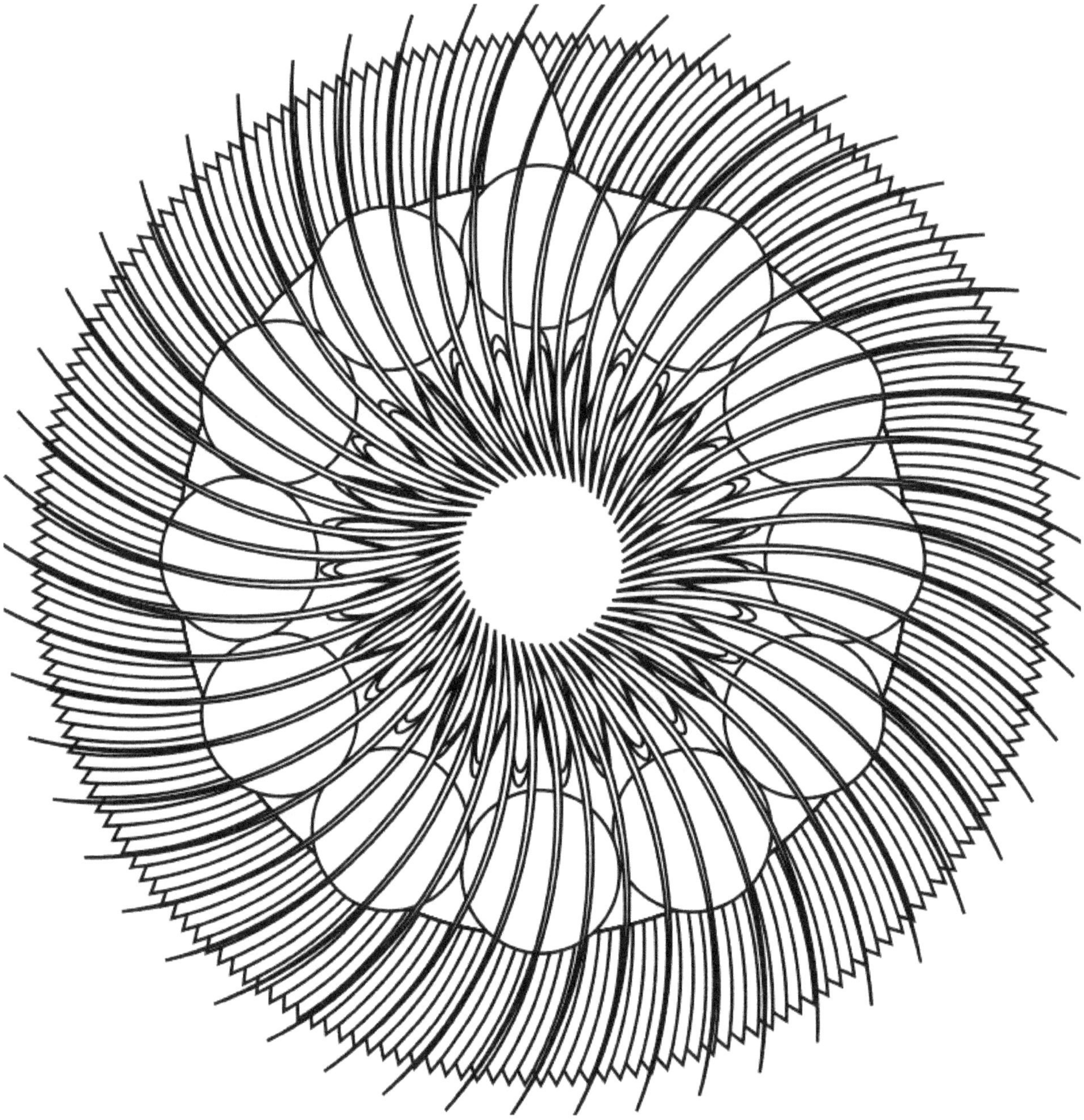

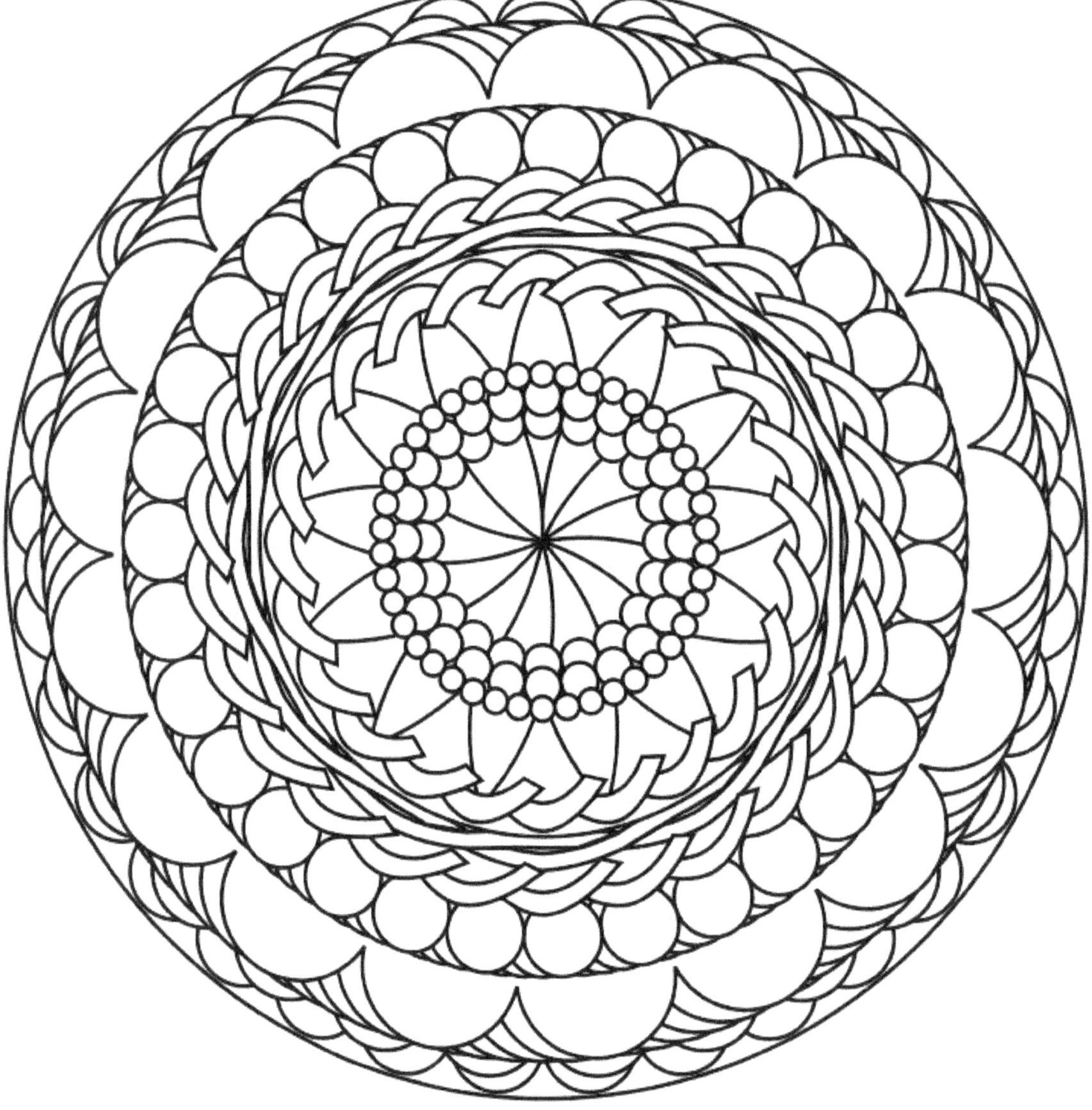

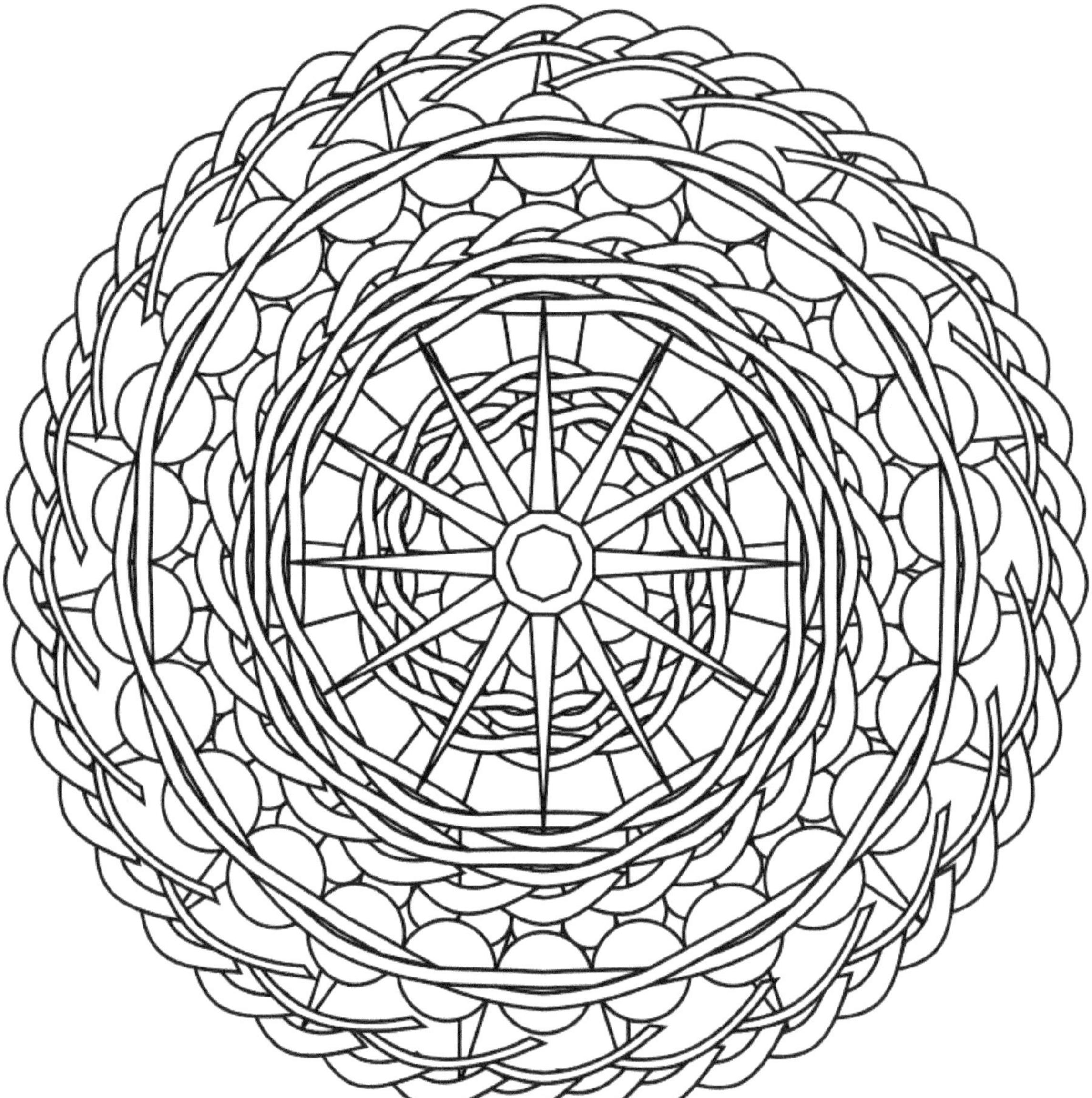

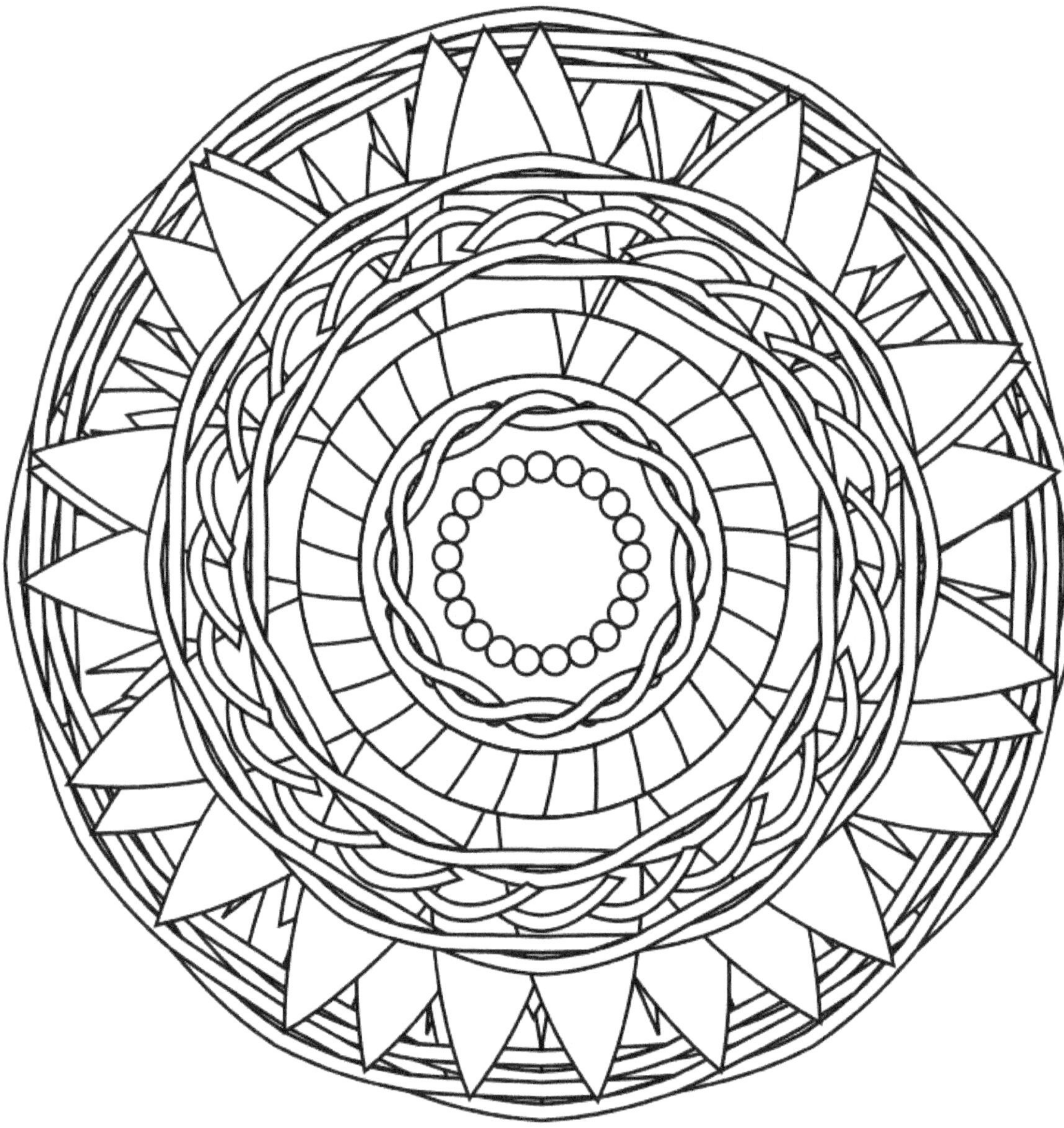

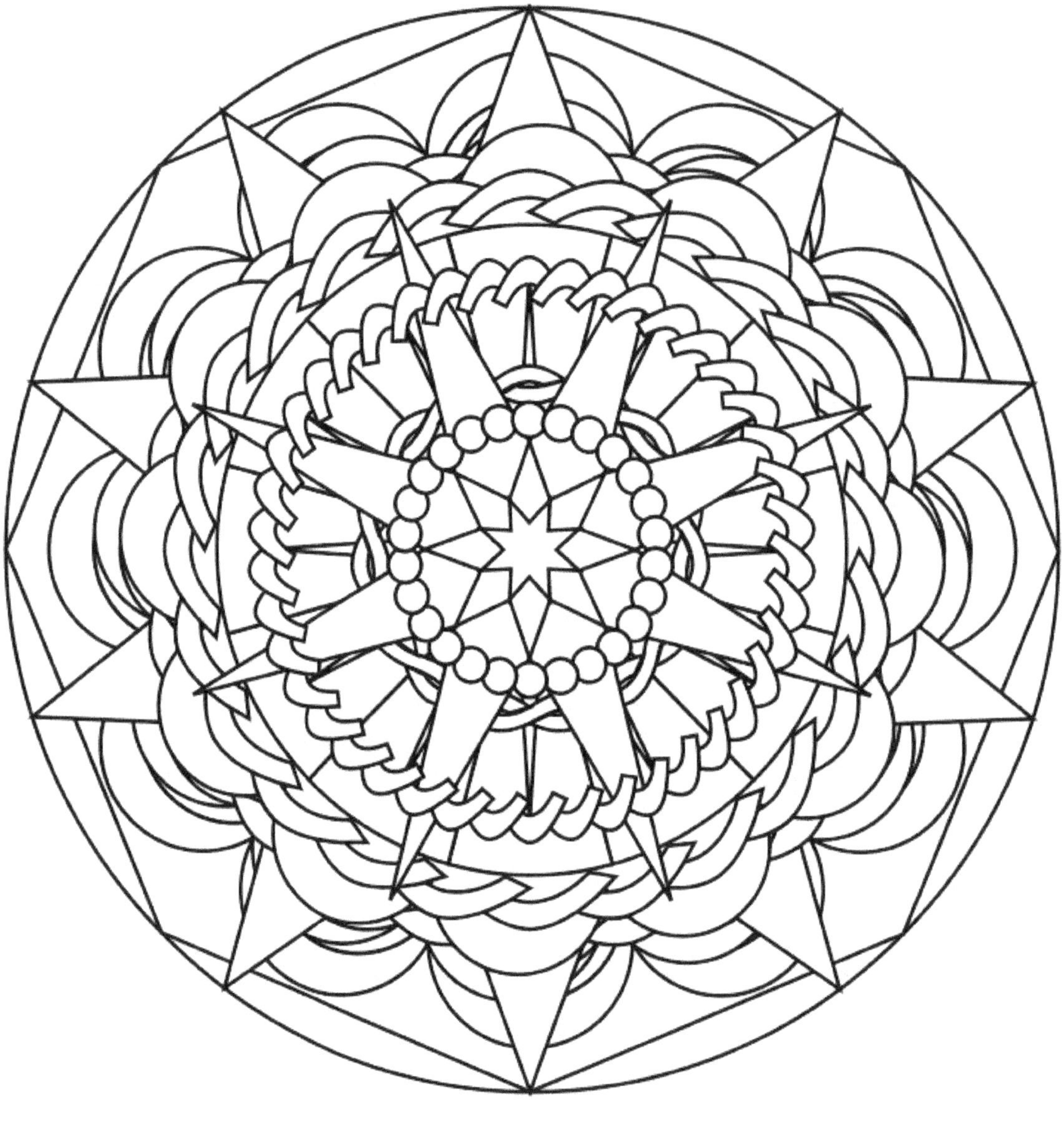

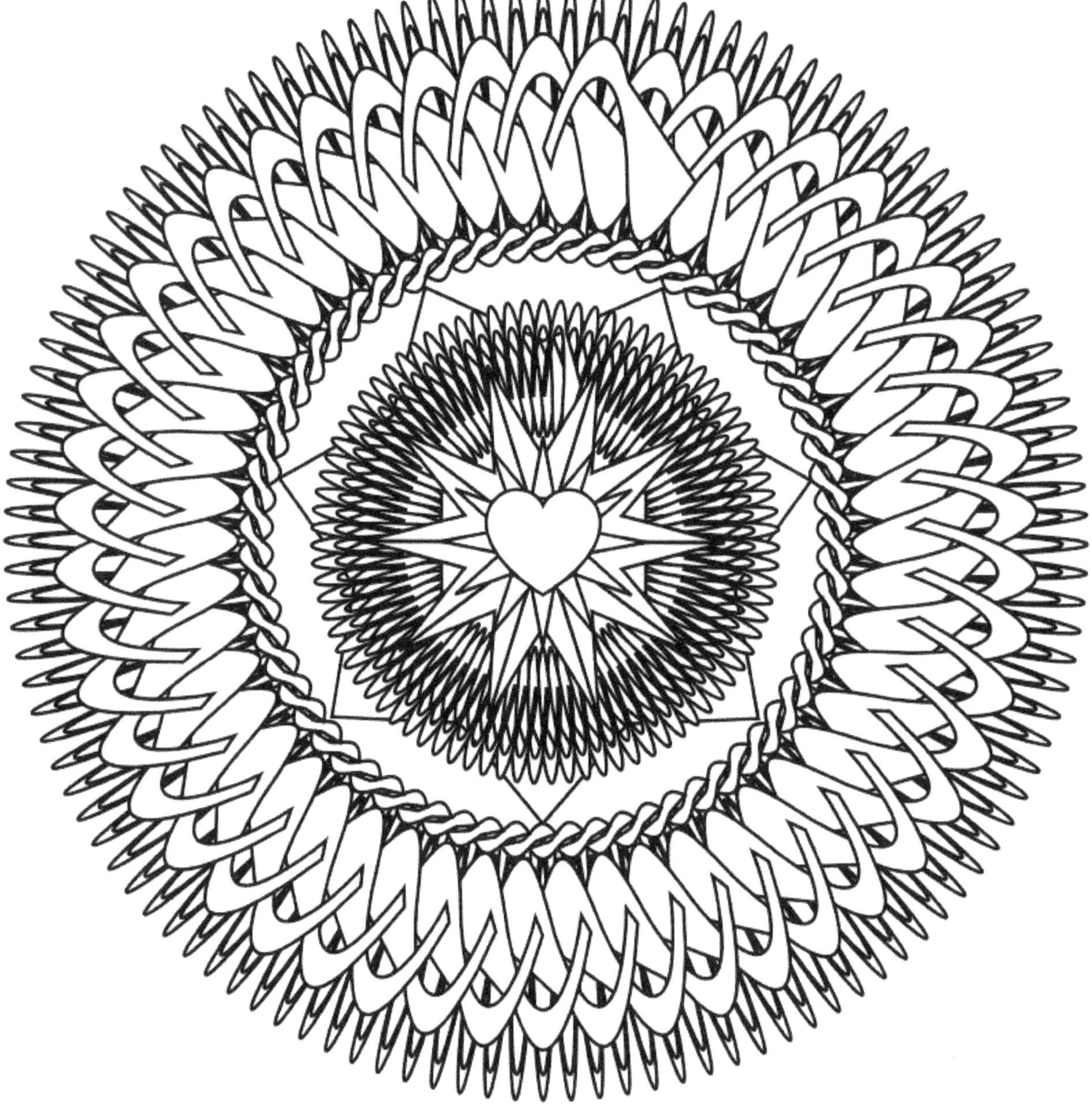

www.ingramcontent.com/pod-product-compliance
Lightning Source LLC
Chambersburg PA
CBHW081308180526
45170CB00007B/2610
* 9 7 8 1 5 2 2 9 1 2 1 3 2 *